# PRAISE
## My Key To A High Place

---

Emmanuel Olowokere

PRAISE: MY KEY TO A HIGH PLACE
Copyright © 2014 by Pray Network Incorporated

All rights reserved. No part of this book may be reproduced or transmitted in any form or by any means without written permission from the author.

ISBN 978-0-9914852-3-9

## Dedication

This Book is dedicated to our Lord God Almighty, the one from whom all blessings flow, the one that makes all things good in his time. To you be all the glory, Lord.

## Table of Contents

Foreword Pastor E.A. Adeboye ...................... 5

Preface ........................................................... 7

Introduction .................................................... 9

Chapter 1 ...................................................... 13

Chapter 2 ...................................................... 17

Chapter 3 ...................................................... 21

Chapter 4 ...................................................... 45

Chapter 5 ...................................................... 85

## Foreword

The power of praise is awesome; incomprehensible by man. It grants full access to God's storehouse of great provision, protection, mercy and favor. David in Psalm 100:4 said *I will enter the Lord's gate with thanksgiving in my heart. I will enter His courts with praise.* Praise is indeed the key to God's High Place, His courtyard. To dwell in the presence of God, praise and thanksgiving must be your normal state regardless of your circumstances.

Job, who had just suffered total loss of everything and everyone precious, in a rapid sequence of obliterating attacks from the very depths of hell, responded in the most extra ordinary manner. He said *the Lord giveth and the Lord taketh away, blessed be the name* of *the Lord.* He blessed the name of the Lord. By so doing Job took control of the tragedy and wrought a favorable outcome. At the end of the encounter, the Lord restored Job's prosperity and gave him twice as much as what he lost.

The only way out of your present loss, persecution, tragedy or pain is through high praise of the Most High who has the last say. In this book Pastor Olowokere draws our attention to how and explains the various dimensions of praise.

We can and should rise above injustice, imprisonment and persecution. The best way to do this is by Praise. In an orchestrated, false, wicked and painful attack, Paul and Silas were beaten, stripped, chained and thrown into the inner chamber of the prison. They did not moan, grumble or wallow in self-pity. Rather at midnight, Paul and Silas prayed and sang praises unto God. And suddenly there was a great earthquake, so the foundation of the prison was shaken and all doors were opened and everyone's chains were loosed.

If you still have breath, Praise The Lord!

**Pastor E.A. Adeboye**

*General Overseer*

***THE REDEEMED CHRISTIAN CHURCH OF GOD***

## Preface

Regardless of the season, summer or fall, winter or spring, I have decided to bless the Lord at all times. David said I will bless the Lord at all times and his praise shall continually be in my mouth.

No matter what season we are in, God's praise must be constant. Unchanging it must be standard, it must remain. "I will bless the Lord at all times and his praise shall continually be in my mouth". When you loose out of praise, you loose out of your raise. Where God's praise is, the bible says that is where he commands his blessings. When you are looking for God's blessings, you find it in the place of praise. You cannot find his blessings where his praise is not strong. "Let the people praise thee oh God. Let all the people praise thee. Let the people praise thee oh God, then shall the earth yield its increase and God, even our own God will bless us and the whole earth will fear him". Psalm 67:5-8.

Praise is not a required duty. It is a living duty. Praise is not program bound but life bound. Praise is not what we do to while away time at the beginning of the service while waiting for the man of God, but rather it is mandatory for the living. The Bible says the living shall praise thee as I do this day. A day without praise is a dead day for you as far as God is concerned. Physicians and others in the medical world, have indicators to check whether someone is living. They check your blood pressure, temperature, and breathing. But as far as God is concerned, the only evidence of your living is in your praises. 'Let everything that has breath praise the Lord"

Praise is the greatest indicator to God that you are alive. That is why the scripture says the grave cannot praise him, so he does not expect praise from the grave. Praise is the mystery behind the rising of Lazarus. It occurred because Jesus took praise to where praise was not usually found. Whenever you praise him, heaven activates these dimensions of liftings for you. This is why he says if I, even I be lifted up from the earth, I will draw all men unto myself.

Praise increases you any day. You cannot find a man of praise decrease. God vowed. He said, I will make my first born higher than all the Kings of the earth and in my name shall his horn be exalted for he has known me and he will praise my name. There is no one who praises that you will find at the bottom. Praise always finds a way to the very top. Through this knowledge, God has inspired the writing of this book.

## Introduction

When I was growing up in Southwest Nigeria, it was fascinating to see people *"spray"* money at parties in return, apparently, for recognition or publicity. Simply described, the act involved throwing, sticking, handing (including any other conceivable way) typically considerable amount of money to local bands - Fuji and Juju usually - at functions in exchange for praise. Once the spraying started, both parties would go at it until the *sprayer* ran out of money or a deeper pocket showed up.

The practice of "spraying" was - and remains - a constant at parties. It cuts across social, religious, and economic statuses: The deep pockets, the executives at multinational corporations, business owners, students, and even individuals who may be unsure of the source of their next meal once the party was over, would spray with reckless abandon!

On one level, the culture and act of *spraying and* praise singing speak to how much people - perhaps even undeserving ones - seek recognition. On another level, the practice speaks to the power of praise and its impact on both the praised and the *praiser.* Praising fosters a symbiotic relationship where involved parties satisfy a particular need, desire or longing. This second level underscores the subject of this work. The major difference is that here we focus on praising the Almighty God.

God, as the Creator of the heavens and the earth, and the preserver of life, at a minimum, deserves recognition and adulation for *"spraying"* you with life and attendant goodies. Like the local bands in southwest Nigeria, you would be wise to eulogize Him ceaselessly. The great part of this is, unlike the praised in Nigeria, you could never bankrupt God since He created and owns all things.

As good as it is to praise God for "spraying" you with life and its riches, it is even better when you laud Him simply for who He is. This is an open secret seasoned "praisers" have figured. These individuals understand that when you selflessly praise another, the praised gets the message and rewards you anyway. The same applies with God. When you praise God just for that sake, He rewards your effort in ways you could never imagine.

This book comprises five chapters. The first, "Understanding Praise", lays the foundation for appreciating "praise". "Why Praise?" the second chapter, provides an understanding of the need and the reward of praise. The third Chapter explores "Brands of Praise". Yada, Zamar, Hilah, Mahalal and Eucharisten are some examples of these brands. The fourth chapter centers on the "Forms of Praise". It lays out other realizations of praise such as testimony, thanksgiving, vow and adoration. "The Works of Praise" in

Chapter five completes the book. It covers the role of praise as a weapon of warfare and how we manifest God's glory through praise.

# Chapter One
# UNDERSTANDING PRAISE

## Praise Defined

We define praise simply as exalting God for who He is and not just for what He does. It is the act of acclaiming, applauding, complementing or hailing God. It is the practice of recommending, raising, celebrating, extolling, glorifying, and magnifying God.

From these definitions, we see that praise is a laudatory act performed to God without the expectation of reward. This means that one should praise God independent of expected benefits.

## Praise Derivables

Lexically, the word "Praise" has three derivable words: 'raise', 'rise', and 'arise'. All three words point to the benefits that one receives when one lives a life of praise.

To understand *raise* as an offshoot of praise, let us consider the story of Lazarus in John 11. Lazarus was not just dead; he was buried for four days by the time Jesus arrived on the scene. Nonetheless, God *raised* Lazarus from the dead once Jesus gave Him thanks. By giving thanks, Jesus was praising God:

> *Then they took away the stone from the place where the dead was laid. And Jesus lifted up his eyes, and said, Father, I thank thee that thou hast heard me. And I knew that thou hearest me always: but because of the people which stand by I said it, that they may believe*

*that thou hast sent Me. And when he thus had spoken, he cried with a loud voice, Lazarus, come forth. (John 11:41-43)*

Psalm 67:5-7 shows how *"rise"* results from praising.

*Let the people praise thee, O God; Let all the people praise thee. Then the earth shall yield her increase; and God, even our own God, shall bless us. (Psalm 67:5-6)*

When "the people" praise God, the earth yields her increase as God's blessing flow to the people in return. This causes the praiser(s) to rise (increase).

The third derivable, *arise*, occurs when God arises on behalf of His people. We see this exemplified well in *Isaiah 60:1 and Joshua 6*.

## Praise: Expected of Every Living

*Psalm 150:6* enjoins everything that has breath to praise the Lord because the only place God is not expecting praise is the grave. To stay out of the grave then, we must stay in praise. We must form a habit of and maintain an attitude of praise. It must be a lifestyle and not a doctrine or a church program.

As you read this book, may God inspire you to cultivate a new attitude of praise in Jesus name. Amen.

## Chapter Two
## WHY PRAISE

Knowing what to do in any given situation is a huge step toward success. If you have ever seen a visitor at a crossroads or a newbie at work, you would appreciate the place of expertise or knowledge in success. Similarly, unless one is praise-savvy, there is no telling the extent of one's loss. The story of the ten lepers who came to Jesus in Luke 17:12-19 illustrates this well:

*And as he entered into a certain village, there met him ten men that were lepers, which stood afar off: And they lifted up their voices, and said, Jesus, Master, have mercy on us. And when he saw them, he said unto them, Go shew yourselves unto the priests. And it came to pass, that, as they went, they were cleansed. And one of them, when he saw that he was healed, turned back, and with a loud voice glorified God, And fell down on his face at his feet, giving him thanks: and he was a Samaritan. And Jesus answering said, Were there not ten cleansed? but where are the nine? There are not found that returned to give glory to God, save this stranger. And he said unto him, Arise, go thy way: thy faith hath made thee whole.*

Whereas ten lepers came to Jesus for healing, He merely healed nine but the tenth got a tack-on: Jesus made him "whole", because he was praise-savvy.

You must understand that praise is a spiritual catalyst that speeds up the rate of spiritual reactions. When you offer praise, God speeds up interventions in your life and situations.

Psalm 22:3 states *"But thou art holy, O thou that inhabitest the praises of Israel"*. Since God inhabits the praises of his people, you need to know that your praise provides a home for God that then guarantees your place before Him. It shouldn't be difficult to understand this if you understand the spiritual principle of sowing and reaping as espoused in Galatians 6:7: *"Be not deceived; God is not mocked:"* it starts with *"for whatsoever a man soweth, that shall he also reap."* When you *sow* a place for God through your praise, God consequently affords you a place in His presence. The reverse is equally true as 1 Samuel 2:30 shows:

> *Wherefore the Lord God of Israel saith, I said indeed that thy house, and the house of thy father, should walk before me for ever: but now the Lord saith, Be it far from me; for them that honour me I will honour, and they that despise me shall be lightly esteemed. (1 Samuel 2:30)*

The case of Leah, Jacob's first wife, as accounted in Genesis 29, exemplifies the impact of praise. Leah wasn't Jacob's original choice. Her sister Rachel was. Laban was unwilling to have his younger daughter marry ahead of the elder, so he tricked Jacob into marrying Leah. Once Leah became Jacob's wife, she had three sons in succession: Reuben, Simeon, and Levi. In spite of this, Jacob reckoned her second best. All that changed once she gave birth to her fourth son, Judah, which means Praise. Leah's life turned a corner so much so that Rachel, the erstwhile invincible sister-rival, envied her. As if that wasn't enough comfort, the birth of Judah bestowed on Leah a place in the ancestry of our Lord Jesus Christ. Certainly not a negligible *raise* for a woman that wasn't her husband's original choice!

## Chapter Three
## BRANDS OF PRAISE

Praise has many sides or if you may, brands. This chapter will explore these brands. Before we examine the praise brands in succession, please understand that praise is a means to an end. It is a journey to a destination. In fact, your high praise is the highway to your high place.

### *Halal*

Halal is the first brand of praise we will discuss. Halal is a Hebrew word that means to 'make noise'. It implies rejoicing in the Lord with our voice. *Psalm 95:1-3* lets us in on how to do this:

> *O COME, let us sing unto the Lord: let us make a joyful noise to the Rock of our salvation. Let us come*

*before his presence with thanksgiving, and make a joyful noise with psalms.* For the LORD is a great God, and a great King above all gods. *(Psalm 95:1-3)*

Through Halal, we can declare the greatness of God and make mention of the marvelous things that He has done as well as His mercies to us. *Psalm 98:1-3* shows us how:

*O SING unto the Lord a new song; for he hath done marvelous things: his right hand, and his holy arm, hath gotten him the victory. The Lord hath made known his salvation: his righteousness hath he openly shown in the sight of the heathen. He hath remembered his mercy and his truth toward the house of Israel: all the ends of the earth have seen the salvation of our God.*

## *Yada*

Yada as a brand of praise describes the act of praising God with bodily expressions. This could range from facial to physical expressions like dancing, kneeling, and lying down, while praising God. Psalm 149:1-3 and 150:1-6 refer to Yada:

> *PRAISE YE the Lord. Sing unto the Lord a new song, and his praise in the congregation of saints. Let Israel rejoice in him that made him: let the children of Zion be joyful in their King. Let them praise his name in the dance: let them sing praises unto him with the timbrel and harp (Psalm 149: 1-3).*

> *Praise YE the Lord. Praise God in his sanctuary: praise him in the firmament of his power. Praise him for his mighty acts; praise him according to his*

*excellent greatness. Praise him with the sound of the trumpet: praise him with the psaltery and harp. Praise him with the timbrel and dance: praise him with stringed instruments and organs. Praise him upon the high-sounding cymbals. Let everything that hath breath praise the Lord. Praise ye the Lord (Psalm 150:1-6)*

David Yada*ed* God when he relocated the Ark of God to the City of David. He danced so much that his wife Michal regarded him with disdain to the displeasure of God. For her disdain, God made Michal the only barren woman that existed in the Bible. She was never relieved of her barrenness:

*And David danced before the Lord with all his might; and David was girded with a linen ephod. So David and all the house of Israel brought up the ark of the Lord with shouting, and with the sound of the trumpet. And as the ark of the Lord came into the city of David,*

*Michal Saul's daughter looked through a window, and saw king David leaping and dancing before the Lord; and she despised him in her heart...Then David returned to bless his household. And Michal the daughter of Saul came out to meet David, and said, How glorious was the king of Israel today, who uncovered himself to day in the eyes of the handmaids of his servants, as one of the vain fellows shamelessly uncovereth himself! And David said unto Michal, It was before the LORD, which chose me before thy father, and before all his house, to appoint me ruler over the people of the LORD, over Israel: therefore will I play before the LORD. And I will yet be more vile than thus, and will be base in mine own sight: and of the maidservants which thou hast spoken of, of them shall I be had in honor. Therefore Michal the daughter of Saul had no child unto the day of her death. (2 Samuel 6:14-16; 20-23).*

Judging from Michal's experience, God desires us to harbor no restraint in Yada*ing* Him. Absolutely no fear or concern of other people's thoughts and attitudes should matter. Jeremiah 31:13-14 further suggests that praising God with bodily expression should not be limited to particular individuals or age groups. It should apply across board:

> *Then shall the virgin, rejoice in the dance, both young men and old together: for I will turn their mourning into joy, and will comfort them, and make them rejoice from their sorrow. And I will satiate the soul of the priests with fatness, and my people shall be satisfied with goodness, saith the Lord (Jeremiah 31:13-14).*

### *Zamar*

When we praise God Zamar style, we praise him with music and instruments. Every living creature is an instrumentalist, because we have our "ten stringed instruments", which are our hands. When we clap in praise to God, we are offering Zamar to Him. Psalm 33:2-3, 92:1-3, Isaiah 38:20, 1 Chronicles 15:15-16, and 2 Chronicles 5:13-14 provide good examples as we see in the following:

*Rejoice in the Lord, O ye righteous: for praise is comely for the upright. Praise the Lord with harp: sing unto him with the psaltery and an instrument of ten strings Sing unto him a new song. Sing unto him a new song; play skillfully with a loud noise (Psalm 33:2-3).*

*It is a good thing to give thanks unto the Lord, and to sing praises unto thy name, O mist high: To show forth thy loving kindness in the morning, and thy faithfulness every night, upon an instrument of ten strings, and upon the harp with a solemn sound (Psalm 92:1-3).*

*The LORD was ready to save me: therefore we will sing my songs to the stringed instruments all the days of our life in the house of the LORD (Isaiah 38:20).*

*And the children of the Levites bare the ark of God upon their shoulders with the staves thereon, as Moses commanded according to the word of the Lord. And David spake to the chief of the Levites to appoint their brethren to be the singers with instruments of music, psalteries and harps and cymbals, sounding, by lifting up the voice with joy (1 Chronicles 15:15-16)*

*It came even to pass, as the trumpeters and singers were as one, to make one sound to be heard in praising and thanking the Lord; and when they lifted up their voice with the trumpets and cymbals and instruments of music, and praised the Lord, saying, For he is good; for his mercy endureth for ever: that then the house was filled with a cloud, even the house of the Lord; So that the priests could not stand to minister by reason of the cloud: for the glory of the Lord had filled the house of God (2 Chronicles 5:13-14).*

## ***Eucharisten***

This is an emotion-based praise. We engage our emotions to express our feelings to God about what He has done for us. We may resort to laughing or shedding tears for example. This is described in the biblical verses, stated below:

*I cried unto him with my mouth, and he was extolled with my tongue (Psalm 66:17).*

*I cried unto thee, O LORD: I said, Thou art my refuge and my portion in the land of the living (Psalm 142:5)*

*And when the chief priests and scribes saw the wonderful things that he did, and the children crying in the temple, and saying, Hosanna to the son of David; they were sore displeased (Matthew 21:15).*

### ***Eulogein***

This brand of praise involves blessing God by raising our hands to Him. Eulogein is a Hebrew word that means *to lift up hands and eyes to God* as if to say 'God you are my only focus, and for all that I am, I give glory to you'. Eulogein is associated with a testimony. We lift our hands in praise to God realizing that only He could have made our testimony possible. This was what David did after he tore a bear (traditionally weighs between 200 and 600 pounds) then a lion (approximately 250 to 400 pounds) in shreds. He lifted up his hands in praise to God acknowledging God as the reason for the feat. When Apostle Paul declared in 1

Corinthians 15:10 that "But by the grace of God I am what I am", he was giving God Eulogein praise.

When we're not quick to acknowledge God as the reason for our victory, breakthrough or blessing, however inconsequential it may seem, we are not being humble. At that moment, pride is keeping us from giving <u>ALL</u> the glory back to God.

We must realize that whenever we get desired results, it wasn't our hard work that got us the result. It was simply because God chose to meet our needs as our shepherd. If you doubt it, I would show you innumerable hard workers who have nothing to show for it. David must have been mindful of this when he effusively stated in Psalm 103:1-3

*Bless the Lord, O my soul: and all that is within me, bless His holy name. Bless the Lord, O my soul, and forget not all His benefits: Who forgiveth all thine iniquities; who healeth all thy diseases (Psalm 103:1-3).*

### *Barak*

Whenever we come before the Lord on bended knees, we physically demonstrate humility and subordination. The praise offered in this position is Barak. We offer Barak either with straight or bent back using our bodies to express our worship. Psalm 95:5-6 gives an example of the Barak praise:

> *"The sea is his, and he made it, and his hands formed the dry land. O come let us kneel before the Lord our maker."*

*Being humble before God makes us enjoy God's kind of lifting.* James 4:10 shows a connection between "Baraking" and elevation for the one who is doing the praising: *"Humble yourselves in the sight of the Lord, and he shall lift you up"* (raise you).

### *Hilulim*

This is a brand of praise given to God as an offering, especially when rendered as a first fruit offering. In

Leviticus 19: 23-24, we see the Israelites offer God Hilulim praise:

> *And when ye shall come into the land, and shall have planted all manner of trees for food, then ye shall count the fruit thereof as uncircumcised: three years shall it be as uncircumcised unto you: it shall not be eaten of. But in the fourth year all the fruit thereof shall be holy to praise the LORD withal.*

Who praises God Hilulim style? The individual who considers himself highly dependent on the Almighty does. The Bible refers to this brand of praise as 'perfected praise'. When Abel in Genesis 4:1-4 offered the firstling of his flock to God as a sacrifice, God found his offering acceptable.

> *And Adam knew Eve his wife; and she conceived, and bare Cain, and said, I have gotten a man from the Lord. And she again bare his brother Abel. And Abel was a keeper of sheep, but Cain was a tiller of*

> *the ground. And in process of time it came to pass, that Cain brought of the fruit of the ground an offering unto the Lord. And Abel, he also brought of the firstlings of his flock and of the fat thereof. And the Lord had respect unto Abel and to his offering (Genesis 4:1-4)*

Similarly, when we offer God Hilulim praise He in return shows respect unto us. Hilulim is typically offered to God first thing in the morning. Before we speak to anybody else, we approach God with our first utterance of the new day. Here's how Psalm 5: 1-3 capture an example of Hilulim:

> *Give ear to my words, O Lord, consider my meditation. Hearken unto the voice of my cry, my King, and my God: for unto thee will I pray. My voice shalt thou hear in the morning, O Lord; in the morning will I direct my prayer unto thee, and will look up.*

We can liken *"My voice shalt thou hear in the morning, O Lord;"* in the third verse to the first utterance made by a little child when he or she starts to speak. That is the reason Jesus said in Mathew 21:16 *"Yea; have ye never read, Out of the mouth of babes and sucklings thou hast perfected praise?"*

## *Towdah*

When we confess the goodness of God regarding our personal life, we are offering praise Towdah style. Here, the praising party gives praises (Towdah) while acknowledging his/her God-derived accomplishments. Occasionally, we can express Towdah in songs or words in the congregation of God's people. The following are some examples of Towdah:

*Enter into his gates with thanksgiving, [and] into his courts with praise: be thankful unto him, [and] bless his name. (Psalm 100:4)*

*The LORD lifteth up the meek: he casteth the wicked down to the ground. Sing unto the LORD with thanksgiving; sing praise upon the harp unto our God: (Psalm 147:6-7)*

*And out of them shall proceed thanksgiving and the voice of them that make merry: and I will multiply them, and they shall not be few; I will also glorify them, and they shall not be small. (Jeremiah 30:19).*

### *Hilah*

Hilah is another brand of praise. This brand of praise focuses on the reputation of God or on the characteristics of His person. It demonstrates God's faithfulness through the fulfillment of the promises He makes to His people. This provides men (His people) reasons to praise him in an excellent manner. This implies that God's promise and the fulfillment of the said promise are important drivers of Hilah praise.

In 2 Chronicles 20:15-22, God promised the Israelites that He was going to fight their battles. In verse 22, we see the Israelites praise God in anticipation of the fulfillment of the promise. Specifically, they praised 'the beauty of holiness', a characteristic of God. To show his faithfulness, God granted them victory from their enemies exactly as He had promised:

> *And when he had consulted with the people, he appointed singers unto the LORD, and that should praise the beauty of holiness, as they went out before the army, and to say, Praise the LORD; for his mercy [endureth] forever. And when they began to sing and to praise, the LORD set ambushments against the children of Ammon, Moab, and mount Seir, which were*

*come against Judah; and they were smitten. (2 Chronicle 20:21-22).*

Similarly, in Genesis 15: 4-6, we see God promise Abraham that his descendants would be like the stars in the heavens in multitude.

> *And, behold, the word of the Lord came unto him, saying, This shall not be thine heir; but he that shall come forth out of thine own bowels shall be thine heir. And he brought him forth abroad, and said, Look now toward heaven, and tell the stars, if thou be able to number them: and he said unto him, So shall thy seed be. And he believed in the Lord; and he counted it to him for righteousness. (Genesis 15:4-6)*

In Deuteronomy 10: 20-22, Moses acknowledged the manifestation of the promise. Abraham's descendants increased from 70 people to multitudes as innumerable as the stars of the heavens. Again God delivered exactly as He had promised. By his acknowledgement, Moses was offering Hilah praises to God for his faithfulness to Abraham in multiplying his seed as the stars of heaven.

> *Thou shalt fear the Lord thy God; him shalt thou serve, and to him shalt thou cleave, and swear by his name. He is thy praise, and he is thy God, that hath done for thee these great and terrible things, which thine eyes have seen. Thy fathers went down into Egypt with threescore and ten persons; and now the Lord thy God hath made thee as the stars of heaven for multitude. (Deuteronomy 10:20-22)*

Also in Exodus 14: 13-16, God promised to deliver the children of Israel from the Egyptians. In Exodus 15:6-11, we see the people give God Hilah praise because He had delivered on His promise. Specifically, they said in verse 11 *"Who [is] like unto thee, O LORD, among the gods? who [is] like thee, glorious in holiness, fearful [in] praises, doing wonders?"* When you give Hilah praise, you speak positively about God, extolling His greatness.

### *Mahalal*

This brand of praise gives the people of God occasion to boast about him. When Psalms 34:10 states emphatically

*"The young lions do lack, and suffer hunger: but they that seek the LORD shall not want any good [thing]",* David makes boasts about God's abilities.

Psalm 44:6-8 gives another example of Mahalal:

*For I will not trust in my bow, neither shall my sword save me. But thou hast saved us from our enemies, and hast put them to shame that hated us. In God we boast all the day long, and praise thy name forever.*

Mahalal praise relegates man and puts God's strength and ability in focus. It makes us humble ourselves under the mighty hand of our God so that He will exalt us (James 4: 10).

### ***Shabach***

If we ever sanctioned exuberance, it is because to give God Shabach praise, we have to do so exuberantly. We extol Him very highly since we are making a statement to other gods that only our Almighty Father is worthy of praise. Psalms 145:1-4 and 63:3-4 respectively demonstrate Shabach praise:

> *I will extol thee, my God, O king; and I will bless thy name forever and ever. Every day will I bless thee; and I will praise thy name forever and ever. Great [is] the LORD, and greatly to be praised; and his greatness [is] unsearchable. One generation shall praise thy works to another, and shall declare thy mighty acts.*

> *Because thy loving kindness [is] better than life,*
> *my lips shall praise thee. Thus will I bless thee while I*
> *live: I will lift up my hands in thy name.*

### *Ainesis*

Ainesis is continuous in nature. This praise is never-ending; and goes on as long as we are alive. Hebrews 13:15 enjoins:

> *By him therefore let us offer the sacrifice of praise to God continually, that is, the fruit of [our] lips giving thanks to his name.*

And Psalm 34:1 states:

> *I will bless the LORD at all times: his praise [shall] continually [be] in my mouth.*

Psalm 150:6 and Isaiah 38:19 respectively are other examples of Ainesis:

> *Let everything that hath breath praise the LORD. Praise ye the LORD. (Psalm 150:6)*

*The living, the living, he shall praise thee, as I [do] this day: the father to the children shall make known thy truth. (Isaiah 38:19).*

## *Aineo*

This is a brand of praise offered to God by either an angel or a man. It is offered on behalf of a person or person(s) based on what God is about to do with them. In Luke 2, we see the angels thanking God on behalf of humankind. We equally see the shepherds praising and glorifying God on behalf of the child Jesus and the salvation of humankind. In Luke 19: 32-38, the multitude of disciples blessed God on behalf of Jesus. Typically, multiple people or angelic hosts offer God Aineo.

## Chapter Four
## FORMS OF PRAISE

Praise as a tool of service to God manifests in many forms. These include worship, giving of thanks, testimony, adoration, making and paying of vows, magnifying the Lord, and blessing the Lord. This Chapter explores these forms.

### *Worship*

We worship whenever we acquiesce and accord an entity reverent devotion or loyalty. It is an uninhibited act that requires the subjection of all else. In Hebrew, worship means to bow down or prostrate oneself in a posture indicating reverence and homage to a higher power. This is why ONLY God is deserving of worship.

Worship is such a potent tool even the devil understands its significance. In Matthew 4:8-10, as he sought to tempt Jesus, the devil asked that Jesus fall in worship to him promising him "all the kingdoms of the world, and the glory of them". Of course, Jesus knew better than to worship the devil so he firmly put Satan aright, "Get thee hence, Satan: for it is written, Thou shalt worship the Lord thy God, and him only shalt thou serve." This encounter emphasizes God as the singular recipient of worship. If we worship any other created being or thing we fall into sin (Exodus 20) because we practice idolatry.

Since worship involves heart-felt communication with and reverence to God, it is impossible to worship God and not hear him speak.

Worship and service are inseparable. Worship is an easy way to figure whoever is worthy of one's service, since we necessarily serve whomever we worship. Besides, the extent of an individual's worship determines his/her place with God. In Psalm 110:1, King David describes a conversation between Jehovah Elohim and Jehovah Adonai. The only way that King David would know this was because he was privy to the conversation. God must have qualified David to be present at such a high-level meeting given his devotion to worshipping God.

*The Lord said unto my Lord, Sit thou at my right hand, until I make thine enemies thy footstool.*

Another important point about worship involves its evolution since the Old Testament. Under the old covenant church, worship was restricted to a designated location. This meant that worship performed outside the prescribed location was unacceptable. To get some perspective, imagine the challenge, let alone the impracticality, of all believers having to go to Israel to worship God today! Since God inhabits the praises of his people, the great danger is that God would not inhabit the worship undertaken outside the designated locations. I can only wonder what might have become of us if praise was still location-tied. Did I hear someone say "Thank God for the New testament"? Today, the qualification to worship is to be a true worshipper (John 4). More important, we are at liberty to worship God EVERYWHERE.

What makes one a true worshipper? For one, such has no location or time considerations. He can worship God at any time. For another, a true worshipper carries God everywhere by consciously creating a favorable habitation for Him. Any wonder God desires true worshippers since such are akin to Him.

Please understand that when worship is only lip-deep we are putting up a performance and are as such hypocritical. And God recognizes hypocrites well as Isaiah 29:13 states:

> *Wherefore the Lord said, Forasmuch as this people draw near [me] with their mouth, and with their lips do honour me, but have removed their heart far from me, and their fear toward me is taught by the precept of men:*

*God equally says of hypocrite worshippers in Matthew 15:8 "This people draweth nigh unto me with their mouth, and honoureth me with [their] lips; but their heart is far from me."*

There is a how-to to true worship. Prayer precedes the actual worship. The worshipper asks God to draw his/her heart to him. This is necessary because the heart of man is the seat of worship - Worship focuses on God's personality and not on His promises. A true worshipper therefore determines to worship God based on who He is, and not on expected rewards. The worshipper exalts God (Psalm 99:5) granting Him the outsized presence He deserves. This elicits God's awesome majesty. Once this occurs, God takes over and the devil takes flight.

In case you still wonder why you need to worship, this should help you. Worship is an avenue to show God that He owns you. How better to demonstrate this than to come with reverence before His footstool. Psalm 132:7 says " We will go into his tabernacles: we will worship at his footstool." Given that worship should abase the worshipper while exalting God, when we come to the footstool of God, we must come devoid of pride.

The benefits of worship include a growing understanding of his workings - the workings of God are his principles, which his word clearly displays - and personality of God. We become confident in the word of God because of our relationship with Him. Psalm 138:1-2 for instance states:

> *I will praise thee with my whole heart: before the gods will I sing praise unto thee. I will worship toward thy holy temple, and praise thy mane for thy lovingkindness and for thy truth: for thou hast magnified thy word above all thy name.*

When we worship God, we are not only worshipping God the Father, but the Son as well. Thus, worship also helps us understand the workings and principles of Jesus. Hebrews 1:3 states:

*Who being the brightness of his glory, and the express image of his person, and upholding all things by the word of his power, when he had by himself purged our sins, sat down on the right hand of the Majesty on high;*

Worship releases the ability of God to make his wonders known, and as a result, there is a revelation of his glory for the world to see. Consequently any generation that cannot worship God can never experience his glory (Luke 19:39-40).

### *Testimony*

This is the second form of praise we will be examining. Testimony is a tangible verification that results from remarkable and accurate evidences following foretold or predicted information. It means to attest, confirm, show evidence, produce a proof, and bring a testimonial or witness. An example is in Acts 4:13-17, where we read about the lame man at the "beautiful" gate. The man had been there for approximately 22 years. Even though he was at the 'beautiful gate', his life experience never reflected beauty. The day he received healing, the people exalted the name of Jesus. In spite of the fact that the Rulers and Scribes forbade preaching the name of Jesus, the people affirmed that the miracle that had happened was tangible and undeniable. From this story, we see that testimonies serve as avenues through which God expresses his power. In the same way, miracles are avenues for man to experience the power of God. Thus, as God expresses his power, it is man that enjoys that power.

The Scriptures describe five instances of testimony. The first instance is the tablet containing the law that Moses received. God gave the stone to Moses as the proof and testimony of his law.

*And he gave unto Moses, when he had made an end of communing with him upon mount Sinai, two tables of testimony, tables of stone, written with the finger of God. (Exodus 31:18)*

When God wrote the law on tables of stone, those tables became testimonies. Now our hearts carry the law and as such, our hearts have become a testimony of God's law. God attended to David and answered his prayers because David gave attention to the testimony (the tablet of Stone).

This should impress upon us that God meets his people wherever he finds a testimony of his law. Let us look at Numbers 17:1-4 as further proof:

> *And the Lord spake unto Moses, saying, Speak unto the children of Israel, and take every one of them a rod according to the house of their fathers, of all their princes according to the house of their fathers, twelve rods: write every man's name upon his rod. And thou shalt write Aaron's name upon the rod of Levi: for one rod shall be for the head of the house of their fathers. And thou shalt lay them up in the tabernacle of the congregation before the testimony where I will meet with you (Numbers17: 1-4.)*

A divine directive to an individual based on the laws of God is the second instance of testimony. *Psalm 119:33-36* provides an example:

*Teach me, O Lord, the way of thy statutes; and I shall keep it unto the end. Give me understanding, and I shall keep thy law; yea, I shall observe it with my whole heart. Make me to go in the path of thy commandments; for therein do I delight. Incline my heart unto thy testimonies, and not to covetousness.*

The statutes and ordinances Moses gave to the children of Israel is the third instance of testimony found in the Scripture. Here is how Deuteronomy 4: 40-45 captures it:

*Thou shalt keep therefore his statutes, and his commandments, which I command thee this day, that it may go well with thee, and with thy children after thee, and that thou mayest prolong thy days upon the earth, which the Lord thy giveth thee, for ever. Then Moses severed three cities on this side of Jordan toward the sunrising;*

*That the slayer might flee thither, which should kill his neighbour unawares, and hated him not in times past; and that fleeing unto one of these cities he might live: Namely, Bezer in the wilderness, in the plain country, of the Reubenites; and Ramoth in Gilead, of the Gadites; and Golan in Bashan, of the Manassites. And this is the law which Moses set before the children of Israel: These are the testimonies, and the statutes, and the judgments, which Moses spake unto the children of Israel, after they came forth out of Egypt.*

The fourth instance of testimony is the attestation of a contractual agreement between two individuals or groups. We see this in Ruth 4:1-7 when Boaz, in a bid to marry Ruth, wanted to make sure his relative who had the right of first refusal exercised or relinquished the right. The relative gave up the right and the parties had an attested binding agreement as proof. *Verse 7 of Ruth 4* describes the nature and substance of the contract:

> *Now this was the manner in former time in Israel concerning redeeming and concerning changing, for to confirm all things; a man plucked off his shoe, and gave it to his neighbour: and this was a testimony in Israel."*

You and I have the word of God as a testimony. We have it as a confirmation of the oath that God swore to Abraham in *Hebrews 6:13-18*:

> *For when God made promise to Abraham, because he could swear by no greater, he sware by himself, Saying, Surely, blessing I will bless thee, and multiplying I will multiply thee. And so, after he had patiently endured, he obtained the promise. For men*

*verily swear by the greater: and an oath for confirmation is to them an end of all strife. Wherein God, willing more abundantly to show unto the heirs of promise the immutability of his counsel, confirmed it by an oath: That by two immutable things, in which it was impossible for God to lie, we might have a strong consolation, who have fled for refuge to lay hold upon the hope set before us (Hebrews 6:13-18)*

The activities of God through Jesus Christ both in word and in deed constitute another instance of testimony. By acknowledging his destiny while contrasting it with Jesus' destiny in *John 3:28-32,* John the Baptist indicated that all that Jesus did was a testimony of what he [Jesus] had seen and heard from God:

*Ye yourselves bear me witness, that I said, I am not the Christ, but that I am sent before him. He that hath the bride is the bridegroom: but the friend of the bridegroom, which standeth and heareth him, rejoiceth greatly because of the bridegroom's voice: this my joy therefore is fulfilled. He must increase, but I must decrease. He that cometh from above is all: he that is of the earth is earthly, and speaketh of the earth: he that cometh from heaven is above all. And what he has seen and heard, that he testified; and no man receiveth his testimony (John 3: 28-32).*

Revelation 1:2 provides support for John's statement: *"Who bare record of the word of God, and of the testimony of Jesus Christ, and of all things that he saw."*

We see the fifth and perhaps most popular instance of testimony in the public profession of mercies God shows to his children. When God shows us mercies, He does this, so that we can erect an altar of praise unto him for the glory of his name. When we then openly acknowledge these mercies (testify), we pave the way for God's name to be glorified.

1 Chronicles 16:8 provides an example of testimony as a public confession.

*Give thanks unto the Lord, call upon his name, make known his deeds among the people. (1 Chronicles 16:8)*

It is necessary to understand that we must verbalize testimonies and not keep it in our hearts so that others can hear it, be blessed by it and give glory to God. Psalm 9:11 states *"Sing praises to the LORD, which dwelleth in Zion: declare among the people his doings."* The excuse that "after all, God sees our hearts" never applies since it is what we confess that we possess!

Psalm 18:49 demonstrates how we can use our testimonies to reach an unbeliever. *"Therefore will I give thanks unto thee, O LORD, among the heathen, and sing praises unto thy name."* We must always remember that we are never qualified for any of the miracles that God performs in our lives. Therefore, when we give testimonies, we acknowledge God's power- Testimonies are avenues through which God displays his power while miracles are avenues for man to experience God's power. Respectively, *Mathew 8:1-4, Mark 1: 39-41, Luke 5: 12-15 affirm this:*

> *When he was come down from the mountain, great multitudes followed him. And, behold, there came a leper and worshipped him, saying, Lord, if thou wilt, thou canst make me clean. And Jesus put forth [his] hand, and touched him, saying, I will; be thou clean. And immediately his leprosy was cleansed. And Jesus saith unto him, See thou tell no man; but go thy way, shew thyself to the priest, and offer the gift that Moses commanded, for a testimony unto them (Matthew 8:1-4).*

*And he preached in their synagogues throughout all Galilee, and cast out devils. And there came a leper to him, beseeching him, and kneeling down to him, and saying unto him, If thou wilt, thou canst make me clean. And Jesus, moved with compassion, put forth [his] hand, and touched him, and saith unto him, I will; be thou clean (Mark 1: 39-41).*

*And it came to pass, when he was in a certain city, behold a man full of leprosy: who seeing Jesus fell on [his] face, and besought him, saying, Lord, if thou wilt, thou canst make me clean. And he put forth [his] hand, and touched him, saying, I will: be thou clean. And immediately the leprosy departed from him. And he charged him to tell no man: but go, and shew thyself to the priest, and offer for thy cleansing, according as Moses commanded, for a testimony unto them. But so much the more went there a fame abroad of him: and great multitudes came together to hear, and to be healed by him of their infirmities (Luke 5: 12-15).*

So far, we have been looking at testimony as an instance or subset of praise. We will next look at another instance of praise, thanksgiving.

## **_Thanksgiving_**

Thanksgiving is the act of expressing appreciation for kindness enjoyed or benefited from another. Expressing appreciation for kindness shown will always gladden the heart of the person thanked. The appreciated then becomes inclined to do more for the grateful.

From Scripture we see that struggling with appreciating mortals typically impacts appreciation to God. Why is that the case? *1 John 4:20* provides the clue:

*If a man say, I love God, and hateth his brother, he is a liar: for he that loveth not his brother whom he hath seen, how can he love God whom he hath not seen? (1 John 4:20)*

We can describe thanksgiving as a prayer in which we express gratitude for the divine interventions we have enjoyed. In this sense, thanksgiving is exclusively God's, and we get to publicly acknowledge or celebrate his goodness.

Let us explore some salient points about thanksgiving. **First, thanksgiving is relevant in every situation and for every situation.** *1 Thessalonians 5:17-18 says "Pray without ceasing. In everything, give thanks: for this is the will of God in Christ Jesus concerning you,"* and Psalm 34:1 states *"I will bless the LORD at all times: his praise [shall] continually [be] in my mouth."*

Please note that while we have likened thanksgiving to prayer, thanksgiving in some sense is simply an act of performing God's will while praying. Of course, this does not mean that praying is not God's will. It only implies that God wills that we praise him continuously. When we are not 'in praise', therefore, it is safe to say we are out of his will and out of place. On the other hand, when we are 'in praise', we are firmly rooted in his will and place. In fact, thanksgiving is the only element that makes prayer meaningful to God. That is the reason *Philippians 4:6* instructs us to,

> *Be careful for nothing; but in everything by prayer and supplication with thanksgiving let your requests be made known unto God.*

This means that thanksgiving is useful in all things.

**Second, thanksgiving is necessary at every level of success and achievement**. When we embrace this truth, we commit ourselves to appropriately crediting God as the reason for our successes while discounting our efforts at every turn, however trivial that may seem. For this reason, it is important to celebrate every milestone that we attain. This starts with expressing appreciation for each day. When we complete each day, we should take time out and thank God for aiding us to successfully complete the day. Nehemiah 12:31, 41-44 provides a useful guide:

> *Then I brought up the princes of Judah upon the wall, and appointed two great companies of them that gave thanks, whereof one went on the right hand upon the wall toward the dung gate...And the priests; Eliakim, Maaseiah, Miniamin, Michaiah, Elioenai, Zechariah, [and] Hananiah, with trumpets; And Maaseiah, and Shemaiah, and Eleazar, and Uzzi, and Jehohanan, and Malchijah, and Elam, and Ezer. And the singers sang loud, with Jezrahiah [their] overseer. Also that day they offered great sacrifices, and rejoiced: for God had made them rejoice with great joy: the wives also and the children rejoiced: so that the joy of Jerusalem was heard even afar off. And at that time were some*

*appointed over the chambers for the treasures, for the offerings, for the first fruits, and for the tithes, to gather into them out of the fields of the cities the portions of the law for the priests and Levites: for Judah rejoiced for the priests and for the Levites that waited*

**Third, thanksgiving is necessary for all the acts of goodness and mercy God shows to us his people.** This is described in *Psalms 106:1 and 107:1, 136: 1-3,* which *state:*

*Praise ye the LORD. O give thanks unto the LORD; for [he is] good: for his mercy [endureth] forever. (Psalm106:1)*

*O give thanks unto the LORD, for [he is] good: for his mercy [endureth] forever. (Psalm 107:1)*

*O give thanks unto the LORD; for [he is] good: for his mercy [endureth] for ever. O give thanks unto the God of gods: for his mercy [endureth] for ever. O give thanks to the Lord of lords: for his mercy [endureth] for ever.(Psalm 136:1-3)*

**Fourth, we equally need to give thanks for the supply of all our physical needs or bodily wants since God is responsible for those too.** That is the reason God told Moses, as Romans 9:16 recounts, "It is not of him that willeth, nor of him that runneth, but of God that showeth mercy". *Romans 14:6-7* underscores the importance of being thankful for the supply of bodily wants or physical needs:

*He that regardeth the day, regardeth [it] unto the Lord; and he that regardeth not the day, to the Lord he doth not regard [it]. He that eateth, eateth to the Lord, for he giveth God thanks; and he that eateth not, to the*

*Lord he eateth not, and giveth God thanks. For none of us liveth to himself, and no man dieth to himself.*

Please note that thanksgiving applies even when we experience shortages and lack. Additionally, thanksgiving is necessary in appreciation of the gift of Christ. *2 Corinthians 9:15* says *"Thanks [be] unto God for his unspeakable gift"*

**Fifth, thanksgiving is relevant for the victory we have received over death and the grave.** *1 Corinthians 15:57 says "But thanks [be] to God, which giveth us the victory through our Lord Jesus Christ".* It is similarly relevant to be appreciative for the grace that God bestows on others. In supporting this, *1 Corinthians 1:4* says *"I thank my God always on your behalf, for the grace of God which is given you by Jesus Christ,"* and Colossians 1:3-6 states:

*We give thanks to God and the Father of our Lord Jesus Christ, praying always for you, Since we heard of your faith in Christ Jesus, and of the love [which ye have] to all the saints, For the hope which is laid up for you in heaven, whereof ye heard before in the word of the truth of the gospel; Which is come unto you, as [it is] in all the world; and bringeth forth fruit, as [it doth] also in you, since the day ye heard [of it], and knew the grace of God in truth*

**Finally, we should thank God for the conversion of others from sin unto the righteousness of God.** *Romans 6:17* affirms *"But God be thanked, that ye were the servants of sin, but ye have obeyed from the heart that form of doctrine, which was delivered you."* In the same vein, *2 Corinthians 2:14* suggests that we express thanks whenever we see the gospel triumph and expands, *"Now thanks [be] unto God, which always causeth us to triumph in Christ, and maketh manifest the savour of his knowledge by us in every* *place"*. Additionally, we must thank God for our appointment into the ministry of God, *"And I thank Christ Jesus our Lord, who hath enabled me, for that he counted me faithful, putting me into the ministry" (1 Timothy 1:12)*

### *Adoration*

Adoration is the fourth form of praise we will explore. We see in *1 Chronicles 29:11* that "to exalt" and "to adore" have equal meaning:

> *Thine, O Lord, is the greatness, and the power, and the glory, and the victory, and the majesty: for all that is in the heaven and in the earth is thine; thine is the kingdom, O Lord, and thou art exalted as head above all.*

The New Living Translation renders the passage this way:

> *Yours, O LORD, is the greatness, the power, the glory, the victory, and the majesty. Everything in the heavens and on earth is yours, O LORD, and*

> *this is your kingdom. We adore you as the one who is over all things (1 Chronicles 29:11).*

It is noteworthy that the features and the reason for each form of praise are the major distinguishing elements of the different forms of praise.

Adoration is the act of showing deep, passionate, intense attachment, devotion, and love to the Almighty God for his faithfulness. This action expresses loyalty to God. Given this, we see that adoration as a form of praise makes one loyal to God because, having tried and experienced God, one has proven him. It consequently becomes easy to give one's all to God. This was the case with David as *1 Chronicles 29:11* shows. David had tried and tested God and had found him true, so he was eager to adore God 'intensely'. We see him adore God in dancing and giving. David gave to God with no reservation. For instance, even when God had expressly told him not to bother about building him a house,

David still provided all the materials Solomon, his son, would need to build the house for God.

*Thine, O Lord is the greatness, and the power, and the glory, and the victory, and the majesty: for all that is in the heaven and in the earth is thine; thine is the kingdom, O Lord, and thou art exalted as head above all. (1 Chronicles 29:11)*

Adoration also means to love, have high esteem, have high regard, show admiration, and undertake adulation and personal worship. When you adore God in one or all of these ways, he continues to bless you. This principle is stressed in 1 Samuel 2:30:

*Wherefore the LORD God of Israel saith, I said indeed [that] thy house, and the house of thy father, should walk before me for ever: but now the LORD saith, Be it far from me; for them that honour me I will honour, and they that despise me shall be lightly esteemed.*

If you adore (esteem) God, he holds you in esteem. If not, the reverse applies as Eli sadly found out. In order for God not to esteem us lightly, we must adore him. Similarly, in 1 Samuel 15: 26-31, we see that God rejected Saul because he had first rejected God. He disrespected God by failing to honor his word.

Additionally, adoration, just as worship, has a seat in the heart of man. When worshipping God, we must find personal reasons to worship God. David demonstrated this in *1 Chronicles 29: 17-21:*

*I know also, my God, that thou triest the heart, and hast pleasure in uprightness. As for me, in the uprightness of mine heart I have willingly offered all these things: and now have I seen with joy thy people, which are present here, to offer willingly unto thee. O LORD God of Abraham, Isaac, and of Israel, our fathers, keep this for ever in the imagination of the thoughts of the heart of thy people, and prepare their heart unto thee: And give unto Solomon my son a perfect heart, to keep thy commandments, thy testimonies, and thy statutes, and to do all [these things], and to build the palace, [for] the which I have made provision. And David said to all the congregation, Now bless the LORD your God. And all the congregation blessed the LORD God of their fathers, and bowed down their heads, and worshipped the LORD, and the king. And they sacrificed sacrifices unto the LORD, and offered burnt offerings unto the LORD, on the morrow after that day, [even] a thousand bullocks, a thousand rams, [and] a thousand lambs, with their drink offerings, and sacrifices in abundance for all Israel: (1 Chronicles 29: 17-21)*

### *__Magnifying God__*

To magnify God means to enlarge, expand, and amplify God because we have experienced him. Psalm 34: 1-3 says

> *I will bless the LORD at all times: his praise [shall] continually [be] in my mouth. My soul shall make her boast in the LORD: the humble shall hear [thereof], and be glad. O magnify the LORD with me, and let us exalt his name together.*

The magnification of God should not only come in response to answered prayers, but rather because of our relationship with Him. Psalm 69: 29-30 illustrates this, *"But I [am] poor and sorrowful: let thy salvation, O God, set me up on high. I will praise the name of God with a song, and will magnify him with thanksgiving"*. This means we cannot leave it to momentary spur but must magnify God based on how we experience Him.

The following should be noted about "magnifying God." Magnifying God is a shade of praise that compels you to praise God louder. The more you experience him, the louder your praise of him will be. Magnifying God makes you hold God in higher esteem and increases the significance of God in your life, while enlarging God in your eyes. Our power of imagination about God equally increases. This is crucial to enjoying God as the Magnificent One. This is described in Psalm 35:27, Psalm 40:16, Psalm 70:4, Ezekiel 38: 23, Luke 1:45-48, and Acts 10: 40-46.

*Let them shout for joy, and be glad, that favour my righteous cause: yea, let them say continually, Let the Lord be magnified, which hath pleasure in the prosperity of his servant.(Psalm 35:27)*

*Let all those that seek thee rejoice and be glad in thee: let such as love thy salvation say continually, The Lord be magnified. (Psalm 40:16)*

*Let all those that seek thee rejoice and be glad in thee: and let such as love thy salvation say continually, Let God be magnified. (Psalm 70:4)*

*Thus will I magnify myself, and sanctify myself; and I will be known in the eyes of many nations, and they shall know that I am the Lord. (Ezekiel 38:23)*

*And blessed is she that believed: for there shall be a performance of those things which were told her from the Lord. And Mary said, My soul doth magnify the Lord, And my spirit hath rejoiced in God my Saviour. For he hath regarded the low estate of his handmaiden: for, behold, from henceforth all generations shall call me blessed. (Luke 1:45-48)*

## *Vow*

Vow is the fifth form of praise we will focus on. A vow is a solemn promise or representation by one person or party to another as a bond to act, perform or render some service. A vow likewise means an expressed binding commitment. When one gives up something valuable in order to commit to a future act or promise, where the valuable item is redeemable once one performs the act or delivers on the promise, a vow it is.

It also means to consecrate a thing to a higher power in order to enjoy an expected favor. We see this described in the bible in Genesis 28: 20-22, Judges 11: 30-36, Psalm 22:25, Psalm 50:14, Psalm 66:13, Psalm 65:1.

*And Jacob vowed a vow, saying, If God will be with me, and will keep me in this way that I go, and will give me bread to eat, and raiment to put on, So that I come again to my father's house in peace; then shall the Lord be my God: And this stone, which I have set for a pillar, shall be God's house: and of all that thou shalt give me I will surely give the tenth unto thee.(Genesis 28:20-22)*

*And Jephthah vowed a vow unto the Lord, and said, If thou shalt without fail deliver the children of Ammon into mine hands, Then it shall be, that whatsoever cometh forth of the doors of my house to meet me, when I return in peace from the children of Ammon, shall surely be the Lord's, and I will offer it up for a burnt offering. So Jephthah passed over unto the children of Ammon to fight against them; and the Lord delivered them into his hands. And he smote them from Aroer, even till thou come to Minnith, even twenty cities, and unto the plain of the vineyards, with a very great slaughter. Thus the children of Ammon were subdued before the children of Israel. And Jephthah came to Mizpeh unto his house, and, behold, his daughter came out to meet him with timbrels and with dances: and she was his only child; beside her he had neither son nor daughter. And it came to pass, when he saw her, that he rent his clothes, and said, Alas, my daughter! thou hast brought me very low, and thou art one of them that trouble me: for I have opened my mouth unto the Lord, and I cannot go back. And she*

*said unto him, My father, if thou hast opened thy mouth
unto the Lord, do to me according to that which hath
proceeded out of thy mouth; forasmuch as
the Lord hath taken vengeance for thee of thine
enemies, even of the children of Ammon. (Judges
11:30-36)*

*My praise shall be of thee in the great
congregation: I will pay my vows before them that fear
him. (Psalm 22:25)*

## **_Blessing the Lord_**

The word "bless" in Hebrews means b$^e$raka, which means to bestow good to someone or a divine being as a mark of honor for what the individual or the deity has done. This means that whenever I bless God, I am bestowing good onto him because of what he has done in my life.

In addition, to bless God could mean to glorify him, speak well of or approve him. On occasion, we could bless God with our substance and with the increase of our hands. This may be in form of songs, testimonies or offerings (Psalm 103:1-4, Psalm 34: 1-3, Nehemiah 9:5).

*Bless the Lord, O my soul: and all that is within me, bless his holy name. Bless the Lord, O my soul, and forget not all his benefits: Who forgiveth all thine iniquities; who healeth all thy diseases; Who redeemeth thy life from destruction; who crowneth thee with lovingkindness and tender mercies;(Psalm 103:1-4)*

*I will bless the Lord at all times: his praise shall continually be in my mouth. My soul shall make her boast in the Lord: the humble shall hear thereof, and be glad. O magnify the Lord with me, and let us exalt his name together. (Psalm 34:1-3)*

*I will bless the Lord at all times: his praise shall continually be in my mouth. My soul shall make her boast in the Lord: the humble shall hear thereof, and be glad. O magnify the Lord with me, and let us exalt his name together. (Nehemiah 9:5)*

## Chapter Five
## THE WORKS OF PRAISE

As a living being, we exist to praise God and we praise God to live. Praising takes us to a place of abundance and makes God turn our famine to a well of plenty. This is because where there is praise, God is present; and where God is, there is plenty.

Besides, the degree of our faith determines the degree of our praise. Abraham was strong in faith. It should come as no surprise he was equally strong in praise. Essentially, praise and faith go hand in hand since praise assumes the existence of faith. Hebrews 11:6 tells us that *"without faith it is impossible to please God: for he that cometh to God must believe that he is, and that he is a rewarder of them that diligently seek* him." Thus, we see that through praise, we lift God high and please him.

# Praise as a Weapon of Warfare

## Shouting Praises

Praise is a dynamic tool in the hands of a believer. One way to utilize praise is as a weapon of warfare. This occurs when we shout our praises unto the Lord. Psalm 47:1 says *"O clap your hands, all ye people; shout unto God with the voice of triumph."* As seen here, shouting praises could cause us to triumph in grand style.

## Singing and Praise

2 Chronicles 20:1-25 provides a great example of how singing and praise could be a weapon of warfare:

> *It came to pass after this also, that the children of Moab, and the children of Ammon, and with them other beside the Ammonites, came against Jehoshaphat to battle. [2] Then there came some that told Jehoshaphat, saying, There cometh a great multitude against thee from beyond the sea on this*

*side Syria; and, behold, they be in Hazazontamar, which is Engedi.* [3]*And Jehoshaphat feared, and set himself to seek the LORD, and proclaimed a fast throughout all Judah.* [4]*And Judah gathered themselves together, to ask help of the LORD: even out of all the cities of Judah they came to seek the LORD.* [5]*And Jehoshaphat stood in the congregation of Judah and Jerusalem, in the house of the LORD, before the new court,* [6]*And said, O LORD God of our fathers, art not thou God in heaven? and rulest not thou over all the kingdoms of the heathen? and in thine hand is there not power and might, so that none is able to withstand thee?* [7]*Art not thou our God, who didst drive out the inhabitants of this land before thy people Israel, and gavest it to the seed of Abraham thy friend for ever?* [8]*And they dwelt therein, and have built thee a sanctuary therein for thy name, saying, ⁹If, when evil cometh upon us, as the sword, judgment, or pestilence, or famine, we stand before this house, and in thy presence, (for thy name is in this house,) and cry unto thee in our affliction, then thou wilt hear and help.*

*¹⁰And now, behold, the children of Ammon and Moab and mount Seir, whom thou wouldest not let Israel invade, when they came out of the land of Egypt, but they turned from them, and destroyed them not; ¹¹Behold, I say, how they reward us, to come to cast us out of thy possession, which thou hast given us to inherit. ¹² our God, wilt thou not judge them? for we have no might against this great company that cometh against us; neither know we what to do: but our eyes are upon thee.*

*¹³And all Judah stood before the LORD, with their little ones, their wives, and their children.¹⁴Then upon Jahaziel the son of Zechariah, the son of*

*Benaiah, the son of Jeiel, the son of Mattaniah, a Levite of the sons of Asaph, came the Spirit of the LORD in the midst of the congregation;* [15]*And he said, Hearken ye, all Judah, and ye inhabitants of Jerusalem, and thou king Jehoshaphat, Thus saith the LORD unto you, Be not afraid nor dismayed by reason of this great multitude; for the battle is not yours, but God's.* [16]*To morrow go ye down against them: behold, they come up by the cliff of Ziz; and ye shall find them at the end of the brook, before the wilderness of Jeruel.* [17]*Ye shall not need to fight in this battle: set yourselves, stand ye still, and see the salvation of the LORD with you, O Judah and Jerusalem: fear not, nor be dismayed; to morrow go out against them: for the LORD will be with you.*

[18]*And Jehoshaphat bowed his head with his face to the ground: and all Judah and the inhabitants*

*of Jerusalem fell before the LORD, worshipping the LORD.* [19]*And the Levites, of the children of the Kohathites, and of the children of the Korhites, stood up to praise the LORD God of Israel with a loud voice on high.* [20]*And they rose early in the morning, and went forth into the wilderness of Tekoa: and as they went forth, Jehoshaphat stood and said, Hear me, O Judah, and ye inhabitants of Jerusalem; Believe in the LORD your God, so shall ye be established; believe his prophets, so shall ye prosper.*

[21]*And when he had consulted with the people, he appointed singers unto the LORD, and that should praise the beauty of holiness, as they went out before the army, and to say, Praise the LORD; for his mercy endureth forever.* [22]*And when they began to sing and to praise, the LORD set ambushments against the children of Ammon,*

*Moab, and mount Seir, which were come against Judah; and they were smitten.* [23] *For the children of Ammon and Moab stood up against the inhabitants of mount Seir, utterly to slay and destroy them: and when they had made an end of the inhabitants of Seir, every one helped to destroy another.* [24] *And when Judah came toward the watch tower in the wilderness, they looked unto the multitude, and, behold, they were dead bodies fallen to the earth, and none escaped.*

[25] *And when Jehoshaphat and his people came to take away the spoil of them, they found among them in abundance both riches with the dead bodies, and precious jewels, which they stripped off for themselves, more than they could carry away: and they were three days in gathering of the spoil, it was so much.*

From the foregoing, we see that singing and praising caused a recovery of all that the aggressor-nations took not just from the present generation of Judah, but also from their ancestors. More important, when we employ praising and singing as weapons of warfare just as Jehoshaphat and all Judah did, a fourfold restoration occurs: restoration of what was taken, what was denied, what was unknowingly lost, and what was taken from one's ancestors. The Moabites and Ammonites were descendants of Lot. Lot as we know repeatedly demonstrated ungratefulness to God. Lot's descendants - the Moabites and Ammonites- followed his example and became the enemies of Abraham's children. They had through ongoing hostility toward Judah and Jerusalem plundered them. In this particular case, however, once Judah and Jerusalem resorted to singing and praising, God caused Abraham's children to recover all that had been lost to the Moabites and Ammonites.

## Manifesting the glory of God by Praise

We can manifest the glory of God by praising Him. By "manifest", we mean to show forth. There are hidden talents or gifts already existing in us but they require God's glory to become manifest. Joseph's trying times perfectly exemplifies this (Genesis 38-39). Who would have guessed that Joseph the dreamer-turned-servant-and-prisoner had the wisdom to spearhead the deliverance of a nation as important as Egypt?

When we pray, God desires our praise to precede our request. Solomon demonstrated how this could be done in 2 Chronicles 6. The Lord's Prayer equally exemplifies this truth. That is the reason we see "Hallowed be thy name," a praise to God, in the first line of the prayer (Matthew 6:9; Luke 11:2).

Praise equally results in the manifestation of God through his glory. The prayer of Solomon in 2 Chronicles 6 resulted in the manifestation of God's glory in 2 Chronicles 7:1:

*Now when Solomon had made an end of praying, the fire came down from heaven, and consumed the burnt offering and the sacrifices; and the glory of the Lord filled the house.*

We can also connect from glory to glory by praise. Praising God takes us from one level of God's glory to a higher level. From the Scriptures, we see multiple accounts of God demanding and desiring praise. We can infer that God is obsessed to praise, and particularly craves the praise of men. Although Angels praise God day and night, God still desires the praise of men. In our existence as men, praise is the only thing that we can give God directly. The secret to knowing God is praise.

Let us consider the concept of glory. We can define glory as splendor, majesty, honor, or an esteemed reputation. When we glorify God, we give him honor. To honor means to give high reverence to someone that is highly esteemed so that the esteemed one feels or experiences the effect of the honor. Giving God money should not take the place of giving him honor. It is possible for us to give God money or other forms of offering like our talent, time, and substance without giving him honor. This was the case with Cain in Genesis 4:3. Sadly, in

1 Samuel 2:27-30, God indicated that Eli gave glory to his children above him. In effect, Eli was giving God's glory to his sons. As a result, when Eli died, the glory of God departed from his family.

Given these, we should aspire for a life spent enjoying and experiencing the glory of God, something that can only happen in a life committed to praising him.